# People, Planet, Passion:
## Simple steps to discover a fulfilling non profit career that makes a difference and earns you a living

by Devi Clark

"Know thyself"
- Socrates

To my mother, Anuradha, without whom
this book would never have seen the light of day

ISBN: 1505433487
ISBN-13: 978-1505433487

# Contents

# Introduction: How this book can help you

You know you want an ethical career. You think you'd like to work in a charity or perhaps a social enterprise.

The trouble is, you don't know exactly what role you want, or what you'd be best at. You worry about having the skills and experience that these organisations need. You know that others with more direct experience will be applying for jobs too, and wonder whether you can ever get your foot in the door.

So, although you keep wishing for a new career, perhaps have even applied for a few jobs, you don't feel you are getting anywhere. You crave clarity, a sense of purpose, something you can really get behind to carry you through the discomfort of change.

This book is designed to help you to define the ethical career that would best suit you. You want to find something fulfilling, which really matters, but which also earns you a living.

Perhaps you've already been a volunteer but now want to clarify what paid employment would work best for you. Or perhaps you are in the early stages of exploring fulfilling voluntary roles because you already have financial security and a desire to share your time or expertise.

Though this book is mainly written for people who are seeking to work in a charity, not-for-profit or social enterprise, or who want to start their own, many of its lessons apply to any career changer or first jobber in any sector. After all, understanding what you care about in a career is relevant at any stage or in any sector.

Getting work in a charity or social enterprise can be surprisingly difficult. The job market is competitive. Charities and non-profits are often under a lot of financial pressure and are frugal with the number of people they employ. Even volunteering can take time and be as complex as applying for a job.

So knowing that you are going for roles that suit you is better for you and the charity. You are more likely to be happy and successful in the role, and especially if you are changing sector, why would you go through the effort only to end up somewhere you are not happy working.

It is especially difficult to succeed at a job hunt if you don't know exactly what role you want. More experienced applicants already have a convenient label: they are a fundraiser, an adviser, a charity CEO. Those labels help employers to understand them and make an easy assessment of their qualification for any vacancy.

In contrast, career changers and first jobbers often feel they have to keep their options open. You may feel that you are less likely to succeed if you narrow your efforts to just a few roles.

In fact, the opposite is true. When I hear someone say they have applied for hundreds of jobs and not got any, I am pretty certain that it is the fact that they have applied for so many that has led to the failure. A few, very focused applications that tie in clearly with your motivations, skills and experience are far more likely to succeed.

Knowing that you want to 'help people' or 'save the planet' is a start, but not enough to allow you to focus your energies, create a plan and take action. Neither is it enough to be sure that you will end up doing something worthwhile that you love.

Whether you have applied for just a few jobs in a half-hearted manner, or for hundreds of jobs in a scattergun approach ("surely one of these will get me an interview") this lack of focus is costing you.

So this book is all about identifying what *really* motivates you, unpicking the 'shoulds' that get in the way of your clarity and overcoming the fear that stops you taking action.

As someone who has already made a move from the corporate world to being a well paid employee and now a consultant and coach in the third sector, I can help. I had my own lightbulb moment when I created the space and time in my life to work out what was important to me and I love to help others do the same. I have coached and advised hundreds of people like you to find a fulfilling career or start their own ethical business.

Incidentally, if you are not sure what I am talking about, 'the third sector' is a catch-all term that includes charities, social enterprises, community groups and other organisations with a social purpose. So, working for a charity is just one option – there are many others.

The sector itself has many names: third sector, civil society, voluntary or voluntary and community sector, non-profit or not-for-profit sector. Development charities are often called (international) non-governmental organisations (NGOs or INGOs).

A lot of people don't like the term 'third sector' because they think it makes the sector sound lower than the private and public sectors. I believe it implies that it is a partner on equal terms in making our society and economy function, and so this is the term I tend to use most often.

**How to get the most from this book**

This book is structured as a step by step guide to help you to build your self-knowledge and your credibility. It includes exercises to help you to delve into your own priorities, skills, experience and create action plans.

In the process, I will help you not only to find jobs, but one that feels really aligned with your true purpose and motivation. After all, there is no point in going through all the pain of change only to find you have ended up with something that you don't enjoy.

It is possible you haven't changed career yet because of your own unconscious self-sabotage. It happens to all of us! We procrastinate most when we care the most.

Staying motivated as we face change is tough. So, there are exercises designed to get you unstuck and to identify supporters who will help you as you go through the process.

The only person who can make your career work is you. So, obvious though it may sound, you need to do the exercises!

Each exercise is designed to deal with the very problems that real people, including me and my clients, have faced over the years. They have been tried and tested on real people and shown to be effective.

Reading the book without doing the exercises means you may be less likely to make a real career change than if you hadn't read it at all. Self-help books can give you enough of a 'feel good factor', an emotional boost, that you no longer feel motivated to actually change your life. You need to take action, or you have merely created an illusion of change, but one that won't last.

So, I say it again: please do the exercises. All career experts agree, theory means nothing without action.

**Free Bonus to thank you for buying this book**

Go to www.mynewleaf.co.uk/peopleplanetpassion and add your name, email and the last five digits of your order confirmation number from Amazon into the form.

You will then be sent by email a pdf copy of a **wall chart that you can print out and use as you go through the exercises in this** book. Put it up somewhere visible to keep yourself motivated.

Some of your answers can also provide a focus point as you create a CV / resume.

You'll also be signed up to receive regular articles, podcasts and videos to help you make your ethical career change a success.

**More free bonuses if you write an Amazon review**

I want to know what you really think, and so do other potential readers.

So write an honest review of this book at Amazon, then email review@mynewleaf.co.uk telling me you have and I will send you a link to download five of my past expert interviews.

Listen as:

Becky John, social entrepreneur tells the story of how a personal crisis ended up being the motivation to create her social enterprise *Who Made Your Pants?* which uses offcuts from the lingerie industry and employs refugee women to create high-quality ethical products.

John Williams, author of bestselling careers book, *Screw Work, Let's Play*, talks about making a career work when you don't want to choose just one option for the rest of your life

Steve Preston goes into practical steps to hep you to make a multi-faceted portfolio career work for you

Andrew Roberts, author of *What the Hell are you Chasing?* shares his own story of waking up to realise he was following the wrong path in life, and how he discovered a bigger purpose, and now also helping others to do the same.

Katie Curtin, creativity coach, talks about how to build a creative career, make a difference and earn a living.

# Chapter 1: Starting the journey, making the commitment

*To believe in something not yet proved and to underwrite it with our lives: it is the only way we can leave the future open.*
**Lillian Smith**

Research shows that 80% of people don't enjoy their career and have other dreams. So why don't 80% of us take the risk of making the dream a reality.

I use the word risk on purpose, because fear is the main reason you stop yourself having what you really want. Fear that you won't make it. Fear that when you get there, your dream won't be as good as you had imagined. Fear that it will be wonderful, but that you are selfish or arrogant for having such a good life. Fear of what other people might think. Fear of not having enough money or security. Fear of making a decision that narrows down your options. You name it, you can be afraid of it.

Fear can also drive you to make a change.

One of my greatest fears is that I will live a life without meaning. I am afraid that when I die I will not have not used my time and abilities to make the world a better place. It sounds corny, but it is a deeply held fear.

Another deep fear can drive us to act too. A palliative care nurse once asked her patients about their regrets and published an article and then a book called the top five regrets of the dying. No.1 was that people wish they had done what they wanted more and listened to other people less.

Fear is a necessary and inevitable part of your life. But when it shuts down your ability to choose the life that you want, it is not doing you any favours. So wrest control of your choices back from your limbic system (the part of your brain that reacts to danger) and make choices that make sense to you.

We are going to start by getting clear about how committed you are to making a career change.

## Career Change Exercise 1: How Committed Are You?

Ask yourself now, on a scale of 1-10 where 10 is 'completely' and 1 is 'not at all', how much have you made a commitment to changing your career to something meaningful?  Commitment means you are willing to do the work, get through the emotional turmoil and step out of your comfort zone in service of finding fulfilling work.

There is no right or wrong answer to this question, but the answer can be illuminating.

Go with your gut. Don't overthink. Try to answer what you know to be true, not what you think the answer ought to be.

### Less than 5
If it is less than 5, the chances that you will actually go through a career change is unlikely, unless it is forced upon you.

Knowing this can be a relief. You have permission to put down the idea of career change, give yourself a break and get on with all the other things you are doing in your life.  Feel free to put this book down, or give it away.  Is there something else you are committed to at level 10?  If so, it is right to make that your priority.

If you change your commitment to a new career at a later date, come back to it then.

### Between 6 and 8
This mid-point is interesting.  It sounds like you want a change but have not really made a commitment to making it happen.  This means that you may find yourself giving up, rather than sustaining the action needed to make a change.

There may be any number of reasons for this, and reading this book may help to work out what they are. Perhaps you want more support, or the time is not yet ripe for you.

You could do the exercises and see if connecting to the kind of work that would best suit you helps you to feel a higher level of commitment.

If the answer is still low, fine! Trying asking yourself what would get the answer to be a '10'. If the answer is "nothing, right now" then perhaps you would like to let yourself off the hook. After all, there is no obligation to change career.

And if you find it hard to let go, check in with yourself again. Is it you who wants to change or are you pleasing someone else (or even your idea of what would please them)? What would truly make you feel committed? Can you go for that instead?

You answered 9 or 10
You are ready to get going and this book can help you focus.

Write your answer on the career change wallchart along with the top reason(s) that you are committed to making a change. At times when you are feeling uncertain or fearful, you can use this as a reminder of why you are doing it.

Having really decided to make a change, stuff will start happening. You start noticing leads. You start spotting people who might help you explore what you want. You start being able to take the first steps on the journey.

It doesn't matter if you think these are coincidences that you notice because you are ready or if you believe the universe is conspiring to help you. The point is, the opportunities are there for you to follow.

# Chapter 2: Avoiding self-sabotage

*"But" is a fence over which few leap*
**German Proverb**

Commitment is important, because we all have these times where we sabotage our dreams.

In fact, you will probably sabotage yourself the most when you are going for something you really want.  It is one of the signs that you are on the right track.   It feels very personal, very vulnerable to go for what is really important to you.  It can seem so dangerous that you destroy the change you have already begun to make.

Forewarned is forearmed.   If you start going into self-destruct mode, remember: this is normal.

Here are some things that might happen.

1. Your 'inner critic' starts ranting at you

That voice in your head that tells you  all the reasons that you can't is your inner critic (also known as your gremlin or saboteur). It has known you all your life and feeds you the messages that most press your particular buttons.

It tells you that you are going to fail, that you are selfish, that people will think you are showing off, that you are avoiding your responsibilities, that you won't spend enough time with your children, that you are risking your security, that your plans are too materialistic and not feeding your spiritual side, or too spiritual and not practical enough to earn you a living ....

You get the idea.

Notice the specific messages your voice tells you. When you hear them, remember it is your inner critic and not the whole truth. Speak back to your critic as if they were a separate person. Tell him or her you hear their concern, but that right know you are going to explore these other options. Then refocus on your commitment and why it matters to you.

You can't argue with your inner critic. That voice is part of your habitual responses to new or challenging situations. It knows you too well to have you win an argument with it.

Rather than trying, thank it for the warning, then do what you want anyway. This can take practice, but is very important if you want to move beyond the limits you have set yourself.

2. You feel really tired, all the time.

You know that wonderful kind of tiredness that you feel when you have exerted yourself and you have had some satisfying physical or mental exercise?

I call that 'energetic tiredness'.

However tired you are, energetic tiredness comes with a glow of satisfaction, a feeling of achievement, a sense of progress, fun or connection. Your body responds to that with deep refreshing sleep, so you are ready to do it again.

Even when you push yourself further than you have before, if you do it energetically, tiredness is just part of the natural cycle of exercise and recovery. This is what we are aiming for you to have.

In contrast, 'stuck tiredness' is an energy drainer. It arises when much of what you do feels pointless and hard. It doesn't link directly to the amount of energy you are expending on your activities, because you feel tired whether you are busy or underemployed. It is generated by the feeling of demotivation, overwhelm or stress.

With stuck tiredness you never seem to be able to get enough sleep. To get out of stuck tiredness you may need to do more, not less. More exercise, more socialising, more self-care, eating more nourishing food and taking more action to tackle whatever you are avoiding (such as your career change).

There is one more way you might be tired, and that is when you encounter change.

I call this third kind 'transformation tiredness'.

It turns up in everyone's life at some point, when you move from one part of your life to another. Teenagers feel transformation tiredness as they move from child to adulthood – and, boy, do they need to sleep a lot as a result.

The same thing happens to us all when we encounter change – even change that we desire. Starting a new job, for example, makes us feel much more tired than we used to. Or when we are asked to give a speech to a huge group of people and we just want to fall asleep in the days before the speech. Or if we are entrepreneurs, when our business moves to the next level, gaining more customers and demanding new ways of working.

Anything that challenges us to be more than we had previously allowed ourselves to be, however much we had wanted that 'more' to happen, can send us into a deep kind of tiredness.

It can be disorienting and frustrating, but I like to think about it as a sign that we are like the caterpillar going into its cocoon and getting ready to emerge as a butterfly. In time, as we emerge, this kind of tiredness will pass.

Rather than berating yourself, be kind and give yourself time to sleep and process the new stuff you are facing.

3. The people who surround you may send you powerful 'change back' messages

As you start to go through the steps in this book, be aware that 'change back' responses will happen inside you and the people around you.

A 'change back' response is a sub-conscious (or sometimes conscious!) message that says "this is too hard, let's go back to the familiar."

It may come in the form of a direct verbal message ("Why don't you do what you used to?") or a more indirect push (like a spouse not doing the chores they promised they would take off your plate so you'd have time for changing career).

You may also find yourself resisting these changes too ("It's just easier if I do it myself – then it will be done how I like it").

All of these are normal responses. You and your family and friends feel comfortable with 'the devil you know'.

So if you want to sustain a change, you will need to be aware that this will happen and be armed to deal with it.

# Chapter 3: What do you want; what do you love?

*People take different roads seeking fulfilment and happiness. Just because they're not on your road doesn't mean they've gotten lost.*
**The Dalai Lama**

To find your ideal career you need to find the intersection between what you are motivated by and what you are great at – your skills.

Skills alone don't cut it. Just because you are good at something doesn't mean you should do it. I'm good at folding laundry neatly, wrapping presents and having hot baths. Those examples are obviously not what I choose to base my career around.

But it is less obvious when I say I am also good at creating spreadsheets, crafting fundraising applications or designing basic websites. These are all things I have learned and used in my career (and still occasionally use) but they are not the skills I base my career choices around.

Clearly, if you have no aptitude for something at all, you are unlikely to build a career around it (though please note that Bob Dylan became a world-famous singer), but for most jobs skills can be learned, if the motivation is there.

So, we are going to start with what matters to you most. Tapping into your deepest motivations opens the door to career success. You are most likely to convey your true self and appeal to an employer if you are speaking from a powerful place within.

And the whole point of going through the pain change is to find deeply fulfilling work. Enough of second or third best! We are going to do focus on what really resonates with you. Nearly right has only a tiny fraction of the power of really right.

Then in chapter 6 we will look at your skills, talents and experience. Although new skills can be learned, you may identify talents that point they way to a role you'd love to do. Or you may find that existing skills create a stepping stone to a role that suits you down to the ground.

Ultimately, the perfect career comes at the crossroads of your desires and your abilities.

We are going to start with what you already know

Knowing that you want to work in the charity sector, or that you want to make a difference to the world in some way, is a good starting point. You might even know that you want to work with children, or people with a particular disability, or with animals, or.... you get the idea.

So far, that isn't specific enough to take action.

Most people try to keep their options open. "I want any job that helps people," they might say. But it is actually easier to get a job you want if you get specific. Then you can focus your research, get to know the key people, concerns and language of that role and prepare yourself to be the candidate they most want to meet.

To work out more specifically what work most motivates you is like mining for gold.

If you find it difficult to narrow down the options, don't worry. Start with what you know, because this whole process is about learning and developing your knowledge. By the time you have worked through this book, you will have clearer answers.

Career Change Exercise 2: The Love It List

You are going to want to keep the answers to this question, so grab a large piece of paper, even a flip chart page if you have one or a big notebook that you are going to keep. Write 'Love It List' at the top.

Stage 1: Start with what you already know. Write down here what group you really want to work with and doing what. Put in as much detail as you can (e.g. "doing art therapy with 2-5 year olds with learning disabilities" is more useful than "children with disabilities").

Have fun with this. If it helps you to doodle and draw pictures, go for it. If you want to collage, no problem. Mind maps work best for you? Do it! Or you can find a list from top to bottom. The format is not important, as long as it gets your ideas out of your head and onto the page.

Remember how I really wanted you to do the exercises? If you are reading on it without doing them stop right now. Put your Kindle down. Pick up some paper and get scribbling.

Done? Great. This is your starting point.

Stage 2: Let's go deeper and elaborate on your initial ideas.

Look again at the answers you gave above and pick your favourite one. Answer these questions about it, or add questions of your own. Your answers may be a single word, or have multiple facets. The more facets you can get in touch with, the easier it will be to fill in the picture of what really works for you.

What is it about doing this work that really motivates you? The role? The people you would be working with? The cause you'd be working towards? Being indoors? Being outdoors? The variety? The regularity? The sense of 'giving something back?

There are many possible answers. Write yours near your original love it answer. You might like to use a different coloured pen for the reasons you enjoy it.

If you are someone with more than one idea for the work you'd like to do, you may like to do either the whole of Exercise 2, or even just the second part of it, again.

Feel free to do it as often as you like, whether that be once or eight times.  Each time you do the exercise you will find answers that give you clues to the kind of activities, people and purposes that are important to you.  No matter if they are diverse and complex at this stage.

It might be interesting to notice if there are any patterns emerging, or if perhaps, the pattern is simply that you are a person who likes variety.

Sometimes the patterns will suggest new 'loves' to add to the list and stimulate a new round of this exercise. Sometimes you will find a clear and powerful idea emerges and considering other options just feels like a distraction.

We are going to be using your 'Love It List' throughout the book, so keep it safe.

# Chapter 4: Being your own compass

*Listen. Make a way for yourself inside yourself.*

**Rumi**

Careers advisers sometimes use computer software tools to help their clients evaluate what careers might suit them. The failings of this system can generate rolling eyes and stories from the people on the receiving end.

*"The computer told me I should be a builder,"* says the nurse.

*"The computer told me I should be lawyer,"* says the stand-up comic.

*"And I was told I should work in childcare,"* says the chief executive.

When I started to study careers guidance, I went in having decided that I would never use these computer programmes to guide people.

So, can you guess what happened on the first day of the course? Yes, we were shown exactly these programmes and taught how to use them.

Interestingly, doing that changed my mind about how effective they could be, but only when they are used properly (and they often are not).

You see, all these programmes do is take what you say you like and turn it into something specific. You like being outdoors, working with your hands, creating something tangible – then you should work in construction! Of course, you could also be a sculptor, an adventure guide or have an office job that gives you time to be outdoors in your spare time.

The trouble is, the programme picks the questions and the conclusions. And because each of us is unique, we are attracted to things for different reasons.

One conference organiser, for example, may be good at her job because she loves project management and keeping stuff under control, while another may be good at it because he is motivated by the chance to learn new things and meet new people at each event.

We need a more subtle system that recognises that we are complex, that we change and that we sometimes give the answers we think we should, not the ones that are truly fulfilling. What is that more subtle system?

Simply, it is *you*. The answers are buried within you.

Even the computer system does its best to bring the answers out of you. In the right hands it can do that. The computer system, like this book, is just a tool. A tool which stimulates you to have your own ideas and reactions. A tool which demands that you provide a more nuanced answer than it ever can. A tool that, without your input, is useless, but that can be a starting point for you to explore what matters.

And as you explore, what you are looking for is *resonance.* Wearing your Indiana Jones hat, it is your job to look around the territory you find yourself in, and spot clues to what draws you, what repels you and what just doesn't matter at all.

We are going to do an exercise, this time with two purposes. First, it is going to give you some more clues about the things that are important to you. Second, it is going to show you what to look for when we talk about resonance.

## Career Change Exercise 3: Peak Experience[1]

Think of a time in your life when you were having an intense or powerful experience. It can be anything from climbing a mountain to sitting at the bedside of a loved one. It can be a personal experience like crossing the line of your first marathon or a work based experience like losing yourself in a project that you were delivering.

This experience may have made you feel like you were in flow, losing all sense of time because you felt so aligned with what you were doing. Or perhaps it was when you felt particularly connected with others. Or maybe it was a time you felt truly present, living in the moment.

Your Peak Experience could be happy or sad, joyous or angry: there are no rules about which emotions you were feeling. It is, however, an experience where you felt true to yourself, connected with who you are.

Take a moment to get fully in touch with that experience. Put yourself back into your shoes when you were there. What were you feeling? Where were you? What was happening? What made it so powerful? Who else was there? How did you connect with other people who were there? What else is important about this experience to you?

You might like to write down the answers to some of those questions.

Notice the quality of the energy you feel when you vividly remember with your peak experience. It makes you feel alive and awake, fully in touch with physical and emotional aspects of yourself that can get lost in the daily hustle and bustle of your life.

---

[1] This exercise was designed by the Coaches Training Institute, where I trained as a coach, and is used with thanks.

We call this energy resonance.

Resonance does not depend on whether the emotion is one that we might normally class as positive or negative. We can be resonantly angry or resonantly grieving. Think of the anger that motivated civil rights protesters or the intimacy you can feel when you deeply grieve the loss of someone you love. But, of course, resonance can also be joyous, excited or in love.

You don't have to be extraverted to be resonant. It is about the aliveness that you feel, not the loudness. You can do that with a quiet voice, or even silently, if that is your style. In fact, you could use a loud whoop to mask your indifference or sadness if you feel you are expected to be enthusiastic.

The opposite of resonance is dissonance. Dissonance is a kind of flatness or nothingness. Dissonance is full of 'shoulds' and 'oughts' rather than desire. It is absence, rather than presence. It is depression rather than energy. It is lack of intrinsic motivation.

When you feel connected with your peak experience, you will be feeling resonant. Notice the effect it has on you: on your thoughts, mind and body. How does it change you hold yourself, the tone of your voice, the position of your shoulders? How does it change the feeling of what is possible and what you care about?

Resonance is like the needle on the compass. When you feel the energy of being alive, you are pointing in a fulfilling direction.

As we go through the rest of this book, we are going to use resonance to guide your career choices.

Career Change Exercise 4: Checking for Resonance

Go back to your 'Love It List'. Look at the things you wrote or drew on the list one at a time. Imagine yourself doing them and at the same time check whether you feel resonant.

Do they all make you feel alive? Or did some of the things on the list sneak in because you thought you 'ought' to want them? Perhaps you feel duty bound to include some stuff that you feel responsible for doing, like caring for loved ones or doing the housework.

If you truly love doing the housework (and some people really do) then fine, leave them on the list. If not, cross them off.

We all have things in our lives that we have to get done. We all have responsibilities to others. Doing this exercise is not about abandoning the people you care about or shirking your responsibilities. I am not suggesting that a fulfilling life is a selfish life or that you will never have to do things you don't really want to do.

In fact, a fulfilling life is often challenging and takes discipline and persistence. If you have something resonant on your list, you will want to do it even if is hard or takes repeated effort, like writing a book, practising a musical instrument or organising an event.

Resonance is not necessarily the same as easy. Sometimes it gets you in the flow: a great athlete, for example, seems to be fluid when they move in tune with their body. However, athletes also train hard and pay attention to their minds and bodies.

When we engage with resonant activities, we can sometimes still feel resistance. I find writing resonant, but I still put off sitting down and staring to write. On the other hand, if someone told me I could never write again, I would fight to be able to. I would never want to give it up.

So, resonance is not necessarily the same as ease. Don't cross something off your list because it is hard.

But nor is resonance based on what you or other people think you 'should' be doing. Right now our focus is on what you love. This your chance to focus on what brings you to life.

So go ahead and cross off anything that is dissonant, that makes you flat or brings you low.

# Chapter 5: More sparks to light your fire

*Don't ask what the world needs. Ask what makes you come alive and go do it. Because the world needs people who have come alive.*
**Howard Thurman**

Now you know what resonance feels like, you can use it to add other ideas to your 'Love It List'.

If your list is already really long, or you are already clear what career you want to pursue, feel free to skip the exercises. If, however, you are still casting around, these exercises are a great way to tap into some of your fundamental motivations.

Different exercises will appeal to different people, so you can choose to do them all, or to pick the ones that feel most resonant.

You'll need more blank paper and pens for each other these exercises. As with the original 'Love it List' you can write, draw, mindmap, collage, doodle – or a mixture of all of these – whatever works best for you.

Career Change Exercise 5: Ideal Life Vision

Lie back and close your eyes as you ask yourself this question:

If time, money and practicality were no object, what would your ideal life be like?

Use all your senses, including your intuition, to build the fullest picture you can. What would it look like, smell like, feel like? Who would be there? What would you be doing? What effect would you have on the world?

No editing! Even if it seems like an impossible dream, give yourself permission to keep dreaming it. Impossible is allowed because it will give you clues to what is important to you.

Keep going just a little longer, until there is nothing left to come out. Now, enjoy what you have created. Before moving on, allow yourself to connect with it and take it in.

Now open your eyes and record the most important features of your vision.

What aspects were most resonant? Which parts did you feel you could not do without? What have you learned from this exercise?

Career Change Exercise 6: Role Models

The people who inspire you are like beacons. They prove to us that it is possible to succeed. They provide a pathway to follow, when the path seems unclear.

Choose someone you admire and find inspiring. It could be someone famous, or someone who lives down your street.

This is a good opportunity to use envy for good. Is there anyone you feel jealous of, even if you have kept it a secret? While they may not seem like a role model, it can help you to identify what you crave more of in your own life.

Pick a person who makes you think 'I wish I could do that,' then write down what 'that' is.

What does this person do that you truly admire? Or is how do they do it or where they do it that is most important to you?

Career Change Exercise 7: Play

Play specialist, Jill Vialet, defines play as the challenges that we set ourselves for their own sake.

I love this definition, because I always had trouble feeling motivated by play. I'm quite a serious minded person and some of the things that people do for fun seem too frivolous or dull to me.

But Jill's definition opened doors. She pointed out that a child will sometimes spend an hour or more trying to jump from one cushion to another. There is no purpose in this activity. It doesn't earn money, create a work of art or make the world a better place. But it is fun because the child is testing their boundaries and coming up with ways to meet the challenge.

Human beings are perhaps the only species that continues to play like this beyond childhood.

When we play we give ourselves something to do: we invent a scene and play it out or create a game and try and win it. Play is fun, challenging, allows us to learn, connect with others, develop our abilities... in other words, just like we would like work to be.

So ask yourself, when I have time to play, what do I most like doing? What would I pay someone else to let me do? And what did I spend a lot of time doing when I was a child, just for fun, because I chose to?

Career Change Exercise 8: Compassion Triggers

Those of us working in career change use the word 'passion' a lot. We exhort you to follow your passion.

The origin of the word is from Latin roots meaning 'to suffer', but we don't tend to use it like that now unless we speak of the Passion of Christ. This meaning has evolved into something we care deeply about.

The word 'compassion' also comes from the same root. When we feel compassion we are moved to act, often, by a deep empathy for the plight of others.

Compassion is often a driving force for people who work in the third sector, indeed for anyone who is willing to open themselves to it. Compassion is about being so open and empathetic that it is impossible to stand and watch without being moved to act, even if acting in this way involves personal sacrifice.

This is not a masochistic statement – we do not need to *try* to suffer. Nor do we need to beat ourselves up if we don't suffer – there is nothing inherently worthy about being in pain.

No, what I am talking about is whether there is anything in your life that is so important it is worth true sacrifice, struggle, commitment and risk taking. If you have children, you'll know what that is like. Though special, compassion is an everyday experience for many of us. Why else would you stay up all night with a sick child, even though you have an important presentation at work the next day.

Compassion can be truly tough – challenging us to be our better selves. But compassion is not the same as giving away your power, giving away yourself.

The challenge that compassion brings us is not oppressive, however hard it may be, because passion comes from *your* values, *your* beliefs, *your* inspiration. It comes from a sense of purpose and mission. It is not imposed on us by somebody else, though somebody else's experience may evoke it within us.

Compassion is at the heart of all spiritual paths, the root of forgiveness and the search for meaning. Compassion is not soft and woolly. It expects us to hold ourselves to our deepest values.

So ask yourself, what evokes your compassion? What is so important to you that you would choose to do something about it even at personal cost to yourself? What makes you angry when you see it happen? What tugs at your heart when you see it or hear about it?

The things that are toughest in our lives can also be the things that are the most motivating.

## Career Change Exercise 9: Your powerful story

Human beings have always used stories to convey meaning, to convey identity, to convey truth.

The stories we tell ourselves are the most powerful of all. They can hold us back, but they can also help us find what truly matters to us.

What are the stories that you tell about yourself? See if these resonate with you:

Stories from your roots: Think about when you grew up, what you learned from your family to be important.

Did you gain values like hard work, honesty and justice? Did you learn to care for excluded people, to teach or to experience the joy to be found in sport?

What were the gifts your family gave you, even if those gifts were unwanted? Did you gain insight into the pain of abuse, the grief of being homeless or the shortsightedness of destroying nature.

There is resonance to be found in the joy and the pain of your childhood experiences. What moves you about your own past? What have you buried but motivates you nonetheless?

Stories from your branches: Do your spouse, children or friends lead you to want to pursue a particular career?

One of my clients started a water softener business because when his son developed eczema, a water softener in his own home made such a difference.

Take some time to think and write about your own story.

Try writing it down, long-hand, without editing. Then look at what poured out of you and see what is there. Or see what you chose not to say.

Ask yourself, how has your family, both the generations above you and those younger than you, shaped your values and what you most care about?

Look at your answers to any of the exercises in this chapter, and see what you want to add to your 'Love it List'. Feel free to add things that you are not sure will turn into a paid job. Some of them may do, others may not. Knowing what they are will still help to guide your choices.

## Chapter 6: What do you stand for?

*You gain strength, courage and confidence, by every experience in which you really stop to look fear in the face. You must do the thing you think you can not do.*

**Eleanor Roosevelt**

It is hard to make a career change when you feel that you don't know where your talents lie, you are not sure you are capable or you wonder where you belong.

Belonging is a core psychological need that all humans share, and if you have done all these exercises and still don't know what to do it would be easy to feel down.

At times like these it is worth remembering that if it were that easy to find our most meaningful career, far more people would do it.

Sometimes your lack of self-confidence holds you back from making a decision.

That may manifest itself as perfectionism, which is another way of saying that you are not good enough because you are not perfect. It may mean you are afraid of being judged or believe you are not worthy or capable of success.

In all these cases, the fear of making a decision can overwhelm the fear of staying stuck.

One of my favourite comedy scenes is from Monty Python's *The Life of Brian*. Our hero, Brian, is being pursued by a crowd who believe he is the Messiah, despite his attempts to deny it. He stops at the top of a mound, turn and shouts to the crowd, trying to persuade them to make their decisions for themselves.

'We are all individuals,' he shouts.

'We are all individuals,' they parrot back.

'I'm not!' shouts a lone voice from the back of the crowd.

As well as making me giggle, I think this is a revealing exchange.

If you feel you are part of something bigger than yourself, that you have made a difference to the world, not only to your own life, you can experience something profoundly meaningful. And yet, like the conformist crowd in crowd in *The Life of Brian* it is easy to confound belonging with the need to 'fit in'.

In reality, belonging involves feeling accepted because of who you are, not because you hide who you are. It involves the risk of revealing yourself to yourself and to others.

Fitting in is the opposite. When you fear that you are not accepted as you are, you try to mould yourself to be acceptable, pushing the parts of yourself that you are ashamed of away into the deep corners where nobody can find them.

The world is full of difficulty and struggle. But often the biggest thing holding you back is your own fear of being judged.

Career changers succeed despite this fear. They take their courage in their hands and go for it. Society constantly tells you to conform, to behave, to fit in. But the real world-changers do nothing of the kind.

If you want to change the world, you need to be able to deal with uncertainty and criticism because you are inevitably going to be swimming against the tide, at least some of the time. There is a whole chapter on this in *The Career Motivation Toolkit*.

Standing up and standing out can be personally risky. Humans are social animals, and taking the risk of not conforming is one of the bravest things anyone can do. People will tell you that you are wrong, and you will need to be able to withstand that. It opens you to anger and hate. For some it may even open you to physical attack.

But it also opens you to love from the people who 'get it', the people who care for you, whoever you are.

A few people and organisations have the courage to really go for it. They are not immune from questioning themselves. Nelson Mandela's autobiography, *Long Walk to Freedom*, is full of examples of when he was unsure he was doing the right thing. But he believed he was here to do something important, and his acts were acts of love.

I am inviting you to stand for something. You don't have to be as prominent as a politician to fear being judged. Artists, creative people, entrepreneurs, campaigners and people seeking a meaningful career feel it frequently, because their work is so personal.

My own feeling of being different has led me to work with refugees, to help career changers find where to belong, and to research and write a book about the pain and power of being an outsider. Once I realised what a big deal feeling different was to me, it had less power to run me. Instead, I look it in the eye, claim it as a gift, use it to create the kind of impact that has real meaning.

If you go in with your eyes open, knowing well that your confidence is likely to be challenged and that you can't please everyone, you can prepare yourself.

It is not only politicians who know this to be true. The advertisers of Marmite famously adopted the strapline: 'You either love it or hate it' and based whole campaigns around wooing back the people who had grown up with Marmite, while admitting it wasn't for everyone.

Marmite didn't bother trying to persuade the people who were never going to buy their product. They went straight for their own people – their fans – and did it with humour which allowed those fans to recognise themselves.

And people did engage. They told one another if they were a lover or hater of Marmite. They played with it. And they re-built a relationship with what essentially a dark brown spread with no inherent character.

Career Change Exercise 10: Be Like Marmite

Ask yourself , and your friends and family these questions:

What is unique or different about you, that you are usually tempted to hide? In other words, in what ways are you like Marmite?

Who are the people who love you or find you interesting or appealing because you are like Marmite?

What do you stand for?

When you get worried about people judging or not liking who you are or what you do, how will you remind yourself that it is normal to evoke powerful reactions when you are being like Marmite?

# Chapter 7: Your skills and talents

*As we let our own light shine, we unconsciously
give other people permission to do the same*
**Nelson Mandela**

Put aside your 'Love It List' for a moment while we mine for your skills, experience and talent. Start a new page and have your pens ready.

We will start with the skills that you use in your current or most recent workplace. For example, perhaps you have excellent accountancy, marketing or management skills.

We are also going to think about skills that you might not conventionally see on a job application. Are you a person who always goes round to a friend in need, with a box of tissues in one hand and a box of chocs in the other? Are you a person who plays football with their nephews - and before you know it half the day has gone?

What do you do, at any point in your life, which makes the time disappear?

Career Change Exercise 11: The Skills List

Capture all these skills and attributes that make you special. List all the skills and abilities you have.

Describe these personal attributes in a way that is meaningful to you. You don't have to use job application type language because what we are doing at this stage is mining for gold and meaningful language is just that – meaningful.

Which is more nuanced? 'I am the person who makes my colleagues glad to come to work' or 'I am the person that gets the team to results when it had felt stuck' versus the words 'teamwork' or 'leadership'.

So often people use these generic words in their job applications, but you will never find someone who says they are bad at teamwork, so really they are meaningless. We want to find out who you really are and what you are really great at because we will use this information to find you jobs that make you want to run to work.

The distinction between what you mean by 'teamwork' and what someone else means can lead you in a whole different career direction. So use the language that makes it clear to you – the language that is resonant.

You may find it helpful to pair or group skills together. So, one person might write:

Being a listening ear – providing care to those who need it – being a good friend

Another might say:

Being a listening ear – campaigning to change policy – writing articles that inspire change

Both start with the same skill, but the first person may be suited to caring, nursing or counselling and the second person to campaigning and policy making. Both care about people being heard. Both use different skills and bring about different outcomes.

So, avoid shorthand, job application jargon and go for words full of meaning and insight.

By the way, this is no place to be shy. No-one but you needs to see what you write down as your most powerful and most treasured skills.

Anyhow, holding back is not a virtue here. Hiding your talents is keeping them from the world. You want to make a difference, right? So, let's find out what you are great at and put it to use. List *everything* you can think of as a skill or talent.

Done? OK, now write ten more.

And now another ten. Yes, even if it is hard. Squeeze out those last ten skills, even if it is just that you can cook the perfect boiled egg.

If you found that hard, don't worry. You are trained by society not to show off, and that may go so far that you stop noticing what we are capable of.

If you are concerned that you are going to end up sounding like a contestant on The Apprentice, it's OK! You don't have to spout hot air. In fact, ideally you would tap into the skills you find so easy you may not even notice you are doing them.

Frequently, the things you are best at are also the things you find easy. They are things that get you into flow, so they don't feel like work, even if at times they take practice or demand concentration. They are things that make you feel alive and in the groove. They give you energy, rather than draining you, even if they take effort.

I get that uplifting feeling when I am singing in a group. I feel energised when I am coaching someone. I feel present when I am writing. These are all things that have taken training and awareness, but when I hit my stride, they feel great.

Those are the abilities that you may have discounted precisely because they don't feel like work. If something is fun, it doesn't count, you say. If it is that easy why would anyone pay me to do it? How could I make a living?

Just because you find something easy doesn't mean that everyone else does too. It might just mean that you have found a talent.

If you've found something easy and fun, notice the bright, flashing light that tells you this is something that you should be doing more of. Your ideal work should be enjoyable and get you in a zone where you add value because you are really, really good at it – so good you may not realise it yourself.

If you love playing sport with your nieces and nephews, perhaps you are cut out to be a coach. If you want to also make a difference, perhaps you can work for a charity coaching young people who would not otherwise have the chance to participate.

If you love creating healthy and delicious food, perhaps you could run a community café, or teach healthy and delicious eating, or cater at fundraising events.

## Career Change Exercise 12: That was Easy

Work doesn't have to be hard, just for the sake of it. Can you imagine the wonder of turning up to do something so fun that you would pay someone else to let you do, and getting a salary for the privilege of doing it?

Add to your list the things that you find easy and fun and make you lose track of time, even if you can't yet see how you might make a living out of them.

## Career Change Exercise 13: New Skills

If you are career changing, the skills that are of most interest or use may be those that you have not yet developed. This exercise allows you to include potential skills on the list too. They may become the core of your new job, even if it takes some time to develop them. For example, I went back to university to study careers guidance, which opened many new doors in the charity sector.

Ask yourself, what would you really like to develop if time or money were no object?

Your answer may relate to the skills you already have, but are more directly relevant in a charity role. For example, if you are great at sales you might like to consider developing your fundraising skills. Or they may be new and different, based on an interest you have not yet developed.

Again describe these potential skills as meaningfully as possible.

# Chapter 8: Enrolling supporters

*You are looking for a genuinely supportive person to
help you attain your goals. This person should be someone
you like, trust, and cannot manipulate. Rule out anyone
who will be seduced by your mind chatter.*

**Maria Nemeth**

Sometimes you need others to help you to see your abilities, especially those 'easy' strengths that you dismiss.

So who better than your best friends, colleagues and family to help you spot the things that you discount in yourself? Those are the people that say nice things about you, but can also tell you when they think you are undervaluing yourself or going down the wrong path.

They are positive about you and you believe them.

By the way, these are not the critics in your life. People who tell you things that keep you small are *not* going to help, even if they are doing it because they love you.

Don't pick someone who suggests that you *shouldn't* do something because it is too hard and you might get hurt.

If all you hear from them is that you should stay where you are because change is too risky, even if they mean it for the best, for a career change you need them like a builder needs a nail gun that shoots in both directions simultaneously.

The people you need are the ones who tell you to go for it or enthuse about how well you did. These are the people who energise you and make you more determined to persist. These are the people who believe you can succeed.

If things don't work out the first time, they still believe in you. They give genuinely helpful feedback that helps you learn so next time you do better. These are the people who open you up to a sense of possibility.

Sometimes, people don't offer this feedback spontaneously, but you know they would if you asked them. So this exercise gets those supporters enrolled on your team as you learn more about your skills.

Career Change Exercise 14: What we can't see for ourselves...

Invite one or more people like the ones I've just described to sit with you.

Take a pen and plenty of paper. Tell your friends you are aware that it is sometimes hard to recognise our own qualities and that you would like their help to do it. Ask them to tell you everything they can about what is special about you, your talents, personality, looks... whatever it is, ask them to say it.

Now sit and write down what they say.

Circle things that matter to you most, or that more than one of your supporters agrees with.

There are only two rules, one for them and one for you.

Rule 1: Supporters are only allowed to tell you positive things.

Rule 2: You are not allowed to disagree with what they say, just listen and write.

This is one of the hardest exercises I ask people to do. Do it anyway, because you will learn some important things, which probably include these:

1. Most of those times that you thought people were probably thinking negative things about you, they probably weren't.

2. You have attributes that you didn't notice or undervalued, which your friends appreciate

3. That even though you are blushing and squirming, part of you is secretly pleased to be recognised

4. Some of the things that people say about you will probably jump out as very important to you – stuff you really value and love to do. This is worth remembering.

Don't discount what you hear.  This is what you show to the world and what they truly see of you.  These are real talents that you own and can share.

# Chapter 9: Your top priorities

*A man is a success if he gets up in the morning and gets to bed at night and in between does what he wants to do.*

**Bob Dylan**

You now have a long list of skills. You have listed what you think you are great at, and what your supporters think you are great at. You've pulled onto your piece of paper all the talents and abilities possible, from all walks of your life.

Your skills are key to finding a new job. If you want to be a concert pianist, it is no good if you've never touched a piano.

But you also need to know what skills you most enjoy using. Just because you are good at baking doesn't mean you want to open a café. Just because you are good at listening to others, doesn't mean you want to be a counsellor.

Or perhaps it does.

Some people want to keep certain activities as things they do for fun, in their spare time. If they had to do them every day they would stop being so enjoyable. For others, the chance to do those things they love more often is a boon.

So, prioritising your skills has two purposes. It separates what you are good at from the skills you truly enjoy using, and it clarifies which skills you would like to build into your work every day.

Career Change Exercise 15: Prioritising Your Skills

Take your skills list and a coloured pen. Circle the skills you most enjoy, just like you did with your 'Love It List'. So, if you are good at managing teams, but don't enjoy the responsibility, don't circle it. If you are great at hitting deadlines and love completing work early – do circle it.

Richard Nelson Bolles, author of the classic career guide, *What Color Is Your Parachute*, has a helpful prioritisation exercise that helps you to see which of the skills you have circled is truly the most important to you.

Draw a triangular grid. It should look something like this:

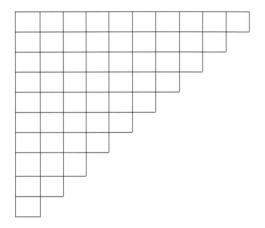

Label the rows with the names of your top 10-12 skills, then label the columns with the same skills but list them in reverse order. By labelling them in this way, each square represents the intersection of two skills – one from the row and one from the column. You should not have any square where a skill is compared to itself.

Take one square at a time. Look along the row and the column to see which two skills you are comparing.

Ask yourself, if you could only do one of them, and had to give up ever doing the other ever again, which would you pick? Write an abbreviation for it in the square.

Do the same again for every pair of skills, filling in every square on the grid. When all the squares are full, count up how many times you chose each skill.

Now you can write them in priority order, with the skills you most want to use at the top, and those which are less important lower down.

When you look at your list, you may start to see patterns emerge, linking to your motivations from your 'Love It List', leading you to roles that you enjoy. We'll be looking in more detail at bringing these together in the next chapter.

# Chapter 10: Discovering your genius

*Everyone is a genius. But if you judge a fish on its ability to climb a tree it will live its whole life believing that it is stupid*
**Albert Einstein**

By now, you are likely to have a long list of things that interest and excite you. Hopefully, you can start to group together the themes.

Do you prefer activities with large groups of people, or with small groups that you know very well? Do you like to plan or to let things unfold? Do you care more about malnourished children, cats, people with kidney failure or those in debt? Do you hate writing, but love numbers?

Look for the repetitions and patterns within your list. Spot the things that come up again and again.

Particular jobs that require these passions and talents may already leap out at you. If so, fantastic! As you begin to research the organisations and jobs that are available, you are now well equipped to assess which ones suit you best.

If you are still confused and finding it difficult to pin down what you want, don't worry. Perhaps you need to do a little more to develop yourself first.

I started this chapter with a quote from Einstein because everyone knows that Einstein was a genius. But they didn't always.

Reputedly, Einstein didn't speak until he was four years old. At the age of sixteen, he failed the entrance examinations for the Swiss Federal Polytechnic in Zurich, apart from the maths and physics elements. In his young adulthood he worked in a patent office.

Not exactly the high flying early academic career you might expect from a Nobel Prize winning scientist, famous for formulating the theory of relativity and regarded as the father of modern physics!

Of course, his career did fly, because Einstein used his genius to do what he loved and was good at. By the time he was in his twenties Einstein was a professor and later a Nobel Prize winner. The fact that his genius was centred on maths and physics, not general academia, became a strength, not a weakness.

We all spend a lot of time and effort on things that are not where our genius lies. Partly it is our school system and social expectations that push us.

We all follow the same curriculum and only get to specialize in our early adulthood. We are told that creativity is important, only to have creative pursuits undervalued and squeezed out of the school day. Physical activity is reserved for those who are good at sports, with the rest left feeling ashamed of their lack of aptitude. But if sport *is* where your genius lies you can easily find yourself written off as dumb. Those development charts that parents read avidly, to check if their child is learning to do the right things at the right time, create needless worry.

In reality *all* children vary from the norm.

Imagine if Einstein had worked hard, into the night maybe, studying to pass exams in literature, history, art or music.

Perhaps he'd have done OK. Many people who put in the work tend to do OK even in the areas they do not particularly show aptitude. He certainly would have gained the approval of his teachers. But he wouldn't have had the time to sit, lost in his own mind, doing the 'thought experiments', which led him to his special theory of relativity.

We often hear stories about high-fliers who are obsessive, sometimes forgetting to eat in pursuit of the thing they are passionate about. Whether they are musicians, scientists, businesspeople, parents, or anything else, doesn't matter. When a person finds what he or she loves to do and is good at, time disappears as they become absorbed in the activity they love.

That investment of time and focus grows their aptitude into ability, and, if it is cultivated enough, into expertise. Then, given space, nourishment and recognition, it is truly seen as genius.

I am not advocating that you forget to nourish yourself in other ways. In fact, getting enough sleep, tasty and nutritious food, creative space and supportive relationships support our genius too. Things that support and strengthen us physically, also support us emotionally and mentally.

Plus, we all have things that we do for others – children, parents, friends, family, colleagues and the wider community – that bring us joy and fulfilment. In fact, it may be the things that we do for others that lead to our vocation.

If, however, those other activities *take over* the space we need to be who we are, rather than *being part of the expression of* who we are, we become like Einstein's fish, fruitlessly flapping its fins at the bottom of the tree. It leaves our life dry and unsatisfying, with a sense of potential unfulfilled.

What if we allowed ourselves to focus on what we truly loved? You know, really focused on it, not just squeezing it into the corners of our lives, when we are already tired from work, from socialising, from child-caring, from anything else that we have filled our lives with.

Sometimes you need to give yourself the time to try out a few of those activities that draw you. Make a commitment to experiencing them, before you make the commitment to a full career change.

See it as an investment in your capability. You are cultivating your genius.

Career Change Exercise 16: Cultivating Your Genius

What if you set aside some real time to do what was truly important to you?

What if you saw that as being vital to your well-being?

What would you discover about your own genius?

Rather than assuming you need to know the answers now and jumping into a job application, start by giving yourself that time to explore your genius. Set aside a chunk of time every week to do something for yourself, to cultivate a talent, explore your creativity, dedicate yourself to being the person you want to be.

If you don't know what that is yet, that's fine. This is an exercise designed to help you learn. You don't need to know the answer before you start.

Your 'Love It List' and Developing Skills list will give you ideas of things you'd like to try.

Making the decision, setting aside the time and acting will open the door and set you on the journey. Ask yourself these questions:

How long are you going to give yourself? Half an hour / 2 hours / 5 hours / a day / 2 days / a week

How often are you going to give yourself that time? Every day / 3 times a week / once a week

What will help you to really do it and not get distracted? (Choose 1-3 ideas)

# Chapter 11: Choosing more than one path

*It is sort of boring to stay in the same spot. You know, I didn't set out to become the first to do this, the first to do that. It was just that my interests were so diversified.*

**Barbra Streisand**

Nobody wants to be labelled. At least you don't think you do.

But when you find yourself with no label at all, that can be equally disorientating. Often, the labels you *like* are the labels you choose for yourself, that you feel describe you accurately so you can be understood and appreciated for who you really are.

A core part of your identity is often based around your work. That's why you so often get to know a new person by asking them what job they do.

With our work comes a label that we can get behind and feel pride in. When we look around and see those doctors, plumbers, journalists, fundraisers, engineers... jobs that people understand and value, we might crave a label too, to help us and others to appreciate our own role and value to society.

Some people are lucky. When someone asks them, aged 6, what they want to be, they already know the answer.

The reality for most of us is rather more random.

Most people fall into their career from a mixture of luck and choices. Career theory even has its own jargon for it: 'planned happenstance'. Essentially, it means that where we usually end up in our career is a mixture of where we are when an opportunity comes up, and how ready and willing we are to say yes to it.

Some of us are lucky to end up somewhere we love. That is usually easier if your parents or friends do similar work. Some end up somewhere they hate, but doing something they feel they 'ought' to do because it is worthy or gives them job security and a good pension. Most end up somewhere that is kind of ok, but not exactly right. Good enough for the familiarity and the security it brings to keep them there.

But for some of us, *none* of the choices seem to work.

Despite much searching, many people find it hard to pick just one thing. If this is true for you, you are temperamentally not suited to doing one job for the rest of your life. You like to do lots of things at once, or one after another in close succession.

None of the options are going to work, because you like change and variety. It is not because you are indecisive. The decision that would work for you is to find a way to build that into your career.

It is easy to beat yourself up for not having found your vocation, for having no commitment or for lacking the tenacity to stick with anything. Perhaps you worry that you are lazy or unreliable. You may judge yourself harshly and fear judgment by others.

Often, people who can't settle to just one thing are not really meant to. You are not flaky, lazy or unreliable. In fact, you are probably independent, opinionated and determined.

You work hard - extremely hard, in fact – when you have fulfilling and varied work. You are warm, generous, idealistic and full of a desire to make a difference to the world. And what you are really great at is learning fast, coping well with change and combining your various talents in creative ways.

The only thing you find truly hard is to pick one thing that will keep you interested for the rest of your life. You don't feel comfortable with a single career label or a single identity. That feels limiting, and one thing you hate is being limited.

As soon as you let go of the assumption that you have to only do one thing, answers start presenting themselves.

Maybe more that one role would suit you better. Especially in the modern age, when jobs for life are disappearing fast, your ability to carry several roles can be an advantage. Why not create a 'portfolio career'?

Is there a label for this kind of person so you can explain yourself to those with more conventional careers? Well, there are a couple, if you choose to use them.

Traditionally this kind of person would have been called a polymath or a Renaissance Man or Woman, with multiple talents like Leonardo Da Vinci or Benjamin Franklin. No one told them off for not settling down and choosing one option!

In more recent times Barbara Sher, an excellent career coach and author invented the term 'scanner' in her book *Could Do Anything If I Only Knew What It Was*. She also set up a scanner bulletin board at www.barbarasher.com and there is a scanner Meet Up Group in London if you want to find others who work in this way.

Alternatively, you could just describe yourself as creative, or an entrepreneur or even not feel that you had to call yourself anything at all! As long as you are comfortable that this way of doing things is perfectly normal, the problem goes away.

There are a few things that can help scanners / renaissance people to bear in mind as they develop their career.

Firstly, you may have a tendency to start a lot of things and not finish them. While finishing everything you start would be a burden, choosing at least some of your projects to finish is important. It boosts confidence and builds your reputation.

Secondly, you will have to go back to the drawing board to learn something new each time you make a change. Rather than seeing this as a problem, remember this is one of the joys of being a scanner! You love learning new things. Being prepared helps you to deal with the financial or planning aspects of making this happen.

Thirdly, some of the things we want to do can take time to earn money, or don't allow us ever to earn enough to live on. You might like to have a bill-paying job to give you security while you pursue your other talents.

Some people who identify themselves as modern renaissance people fit a very diverse range of activities under their career umbrella. How about teaching Japanese part-time while fundraising for a charity that helps stray animals? How about becoming a solar panel installer and also making documentaries about single parents? If you allow yourself the freedom, there really is no limit to where your career might take you.

Others create, consciously or unconsciously, a theme that binds their primary career strands together, even though the activities themselves are quite diverse. In my case, the theme for my work seems to be 'transforming the pain of feeling different into the ability to change the world'.

I have found many different ways of doing this. I organised my university's freshers' week (helping new students belong), volunteered at a charity for homeless people, became a careers adviser for refugees, helped people in a deprived area of London start new businesses, coached career changers to find ethical jobs, became a management consultant specialising in charities and social enterprises which work with excluded people, created a podcast for career change and ethical business start up experts, wrote a book on feeling like an outsider and started a social enterprise encouraging outsiders to believe in their strengths....

The core meaning from my own 'Love it list' has translated into lots of roles using lots of skills and developing new ones all the time. That's my idea of fun.

You don't have to have a theme. Perhaps one of these options might suit you:

Multiple career changes: Become an expert in one area, and then, when that has lost its shine, move in to something new. Notice what your typical cycle is (1 year? 3 years? 10 years?) and start looking out for new opportunities a little before you hit your boredom threshold.

Freelancing: As a freelancer you can have a number of strings to your bow, as long as you market yourself in a focused manner, and are clear who your potential clients are for each piece of work. You might even find one set of customers who need more than one of your skills. For example, a charity that uses you as a fundraising consultant might also like you to design them a new website.

Two jobs in one: Can you find a low maintenance role that allows you to do something else at the same time? For example, what if you earned money working as a night-time car park attendant, which mostly involved sitting and watching CCTV screens and doing the occasional patrol, and at the same time composed music or wrote blog articles?

There are not many jobs that allow this, but if you are looking for roles to support you financially while you do something more creative, you can find them. After all, Einstein did the 'thought experiments that led to his formulation of the theory of relativity while working at the Swiss Patent Office.

# Chapter 12: Your ideal workplace

*When the grass looks greener on the other side of the fence, it may be that they take better care of it there*

**Cecel Selig**

So far, you have been focusing on your motivations (that magnetic pull that leads to your desire to do the work) and your skills (what you are great at). There is one more factor that determines your ideal job – and that is the environment you work in.

I am a firm believer that the person who work for makes more of a difference to whether your job is fulfilling or not than anything else. In my career, I have left two jobs within six months of starting, both because of the boss I worked for.

It is not necessarily because they intend to be harsh. One was a bully, but I believe he thought he was doing the right thing by pushing the team hard. The other was as soft as butter, one of the nicest people I've had the pleasure to meet. But he never made decisions, was chaotic and poor at communication. His team was unhappy and angry.

Although I left that job, I found very similar work with another organisation which I loved. It is often not the work, but the organisation, its culture and your immediate line manger, that makes the greatest difference.

In fact, as well as leaving good jobs with bad bosses, I have stayed for a long time in jobs I didn't care much for, because I worked in a great team with a manager who made me feel valued.

As well as who you work for, and who you work with, where you work can have a dramatic effect on your satisfaction. I had one client who worked in one town, was enrolled on a course in another, lived in a third, had a boyfriend in a fourth and was thinking of starting as a freelancer in a fifth. No wonder she didn't get round to starting her freelancing – she was exhausted about never being home!

Career Change Exercise 17: Your Ideal Workplace

Write down on a fresh piece of paper what you would like from an employer. You can start by answering the questions below, but include any other factors that are important to you

What size organisation suits you? A smaller one is likely to be less bureaucratic and you are more likely to be asked to muck in with a lot of different activities. A larger one is more likely to have structured training and allow you to specialise.

What team culture would bring out your best? How sociable is the team? How do they handle crises? How creative or pragmatic are they? How good at planning vs. how spontaneous are they? Are you office based or outdoors? Are your team thinkers or do-ers?

What leadership works for you? Do you prefer a lot of guidance or to be proactive? Do you prefer deadlines and targets or looser guidelines? Do you prefer to work closely with others or to be out and about independently? Do you prefer your manager to lead with their head or heart?

What location is important? Do you want a short commute or would you happily go further for the right role? Do you want to work indoors or outdoors? To you want to travel or stay put, and if you are travelling is it internationally or locally?

For many of these questions you may want both: a team who thinks and does; a manager who leads with both head and heart. But there is likely to be a way that you lean, personally. A balance that suits your own style.

I spend much more time helping you to define and research your ideal working environment in my next book, *The Ethical Career Guide*, which is due out on Kindle in March 2015.

# Chapter 13: Starting the journey, claiming your future

*Nothing will ever be attempted, if all possible objections must first be overcome*

**Samuel Jackson**

Life is a journey. Making a plan, anticipating problems can help you to be prepared.

But life is also inherently unpredictable. Thinking that you can plan for every eventuality is a mistake.

Things just happen in life: things that hinder (illness, redundancy, bereavement...) and things that help (a promotion or job offer, a supportive relationship, inheriting money). There are as many unintended good consequences of decisions as there are risks.

Let me give you an example. Three years into my undergraduate degree at the University of Edinburgh, I went back to London for the summer holiday. I was writing a dissertation on African Literature and History and I needed to borrow books, so my researches took me to the School of Oriental and African Studies (SOAS), part of the University of London.

I looked in awe at their course options, full of subjects that fascinated me. I wished I had known about it when I filled in my university application forms. They had largely based on guesswork and the experience of my parents.

But whenever I ask myself, with hindsight, whether I would change that original application, I pause. Edinburgh was good to me. It was there that I met the love of my life, the man I would later marry and have children with. I lived in a beautiful city far enough from my family to learn to live my own life. I had many great experiences as well as many tough ones, and even the tough ones taught me life lessons I wouldn't want to be without.

There is a Buddhist story about a group of people talking about the suffering they have lived through in their lives. Each believes that their woes are the toughest to bear. A mystic hears them and gives them the opportunity to hang their sufferings on a tree, then pick another man's sufferings that they would rather take home with them.

So each hangs up their sufferings. Each walks around the tree looking carefully at the sufferings of others. Then each returns to their own sufferings, reclaims them and takes them home.

If you are someone who falls into 'analysis paralysis' you believe you have to work out the right answer before you start, and so you never start.

You can't learn to swim by standing on the side of the pool and planning how you will move your arms and legs. At some point you have to get in and get practising.

Rather than fearing the wrong decision, get in the pool and see what works. Sinking? Then try kicking in a different way, get a swimming teacher to help you or travel by boat instead.

It's fine to stay near the edge of the pool, or at the shallow end, while you learn. But you still have to get in.

Decisions are just decisions. Letting go of the value judgements allows you to move and grow.

Remembering that you learn most from the things you mess us, can free you. You adjust as you go, using resonance as your guide for the direction you pick each time. You go in knowing that you will sometimes make mistakes, just as a child falls down as they learn to walk. So you carry on nonetheless, forgiving ourselves.

How might the fear of making a wrong decision may be affecting you? What you might do about it?

Theodore Roosevelt exhorts you, instead, to 'dare greatly':

*It's not the critic who counts, not the man who points out how the strong man stumbled, or when the doer of deeds could have done better. The credit belongs to the man who is actually in the arena; whose face is marred by dust and sweat and blood; who strives valiantly; who errs and comes short again and again; who knows the great enthusiasms, the great devotions and spends himself in a worthy cause; who at the best, knows in the end the triumph of high achievement; and who at the worst if he fails, at least fails while daring greatly, so that his place shall never be with those cold and timid souls who know neither victory or defeat.*

**Theodore Roosevelt**

Helpful and generous can people find themselves giving away their power to others. They make choices based on the demands that others make on them. Instead, I believe you need to claim your power to make the difference you are capable of making.

Many people who work, or aspire to work, in the not-for-profit sector treat 'power' as a dirty word. I make a distinction between having the 'power to' act versus 'power over' others. Using your power to dominate others is not power: that is oppression. I am a believer in power.

Feeling empowered is important for all of us, and in fact, it is when people feel no ownership of the power that is rightfully theirs that they tend to act out, be they aggrieved teenagers, racial or religious minorities or disgruntled employees.

Power that is not distorted, but is in touch with passion and meaning can unleash wonderful things. Passion for beauty can unleash art, love or environmental projects, but only if you feel the power to do so. Passion for people can give others a voice, tackle abuse or connect us to one another, but only if we all feel powerful. Even passion for finance, which sounds less romantic, can create choices, develop financial security, grow enterprises that enhance the world, giving some of the most excluded people power to make choices for themselves and their families.

Power is the ability to create, to lead, to make things happen. To be successful in your career, you need to own your personal power. To make the difference in the world that you'd really like to make, you need to challenge yourself to be as capable as you really are – in service of yourself and others.

We help nobody by staying small or assuming that we are not important enough to take our place among the people who inspire us.

Imagine if Nelson Mandela or Aung San Suu Kyi had been too worried that they might be being pushy or attention-seeking if they took on a leadership role in their country! Imagine if Plato had been too shy of Socrates to become his student, or Jung had not been willing first to learn from and then to leave Freud. And Adele, with that wonderful voice, aged only 19 - what if she had thought that writing and singing her own album was selfish or showing off?

Perhaps we fear our own passions because we fear stepping into our power. If we own our power, what responsibilities do we have? If we know our power, what commitments must we make to ourselves and to the world? If we believe in our power, how can we sit back and not act?

Perhaps you don't think these points about power don't apply to you because you are just not capable enough. Whether or not you choose to step into your own power is irrelevant, you think, because you have no power. Perhaps you feel you are not smart enough, tenacious enough, lucky enough or simply worthy enough to be able to make your career change happen.

We all have our moments of feeling that we are not good enough to do or be what we want. Here are some ways this might affect you:

You might be trying to be something you are not. For example, if you came from a family where everyone was super-organised and disciplined and you are disorganised and always late, you may feel that you are inadequate and will never succeed however hard you try.

Rather than focusing on the failure, try finding the gift in the way that you *do* operate. Does your disorganisation mean that you always have space in your life for other people, or that you are able to be very responsive and flexible in a crisis? Does this lack of planning mean that spontaneous creative ideas flow from you at the drop of a hat?

Think about it in reverse too. Imagine a person who lived in a creative spontaneous household, but was an organised planner. They might feel inadequate for being staid, boring and slow moving. They could reframe their qualities as reliable, strong and organised.

In truth, almost any quality that we portray as negative could be turned around to show its positive and useful side, as long as it is put to constructive purpose.

One of my small business coaching colleagues had a client who had previously been a petty criminal and was now doing very well developing a legitimate business. It was pointed out the many of the qualities he had developed were entrepreneurial. He was innovative and quick thinking, accustomed to making things happen against the odds. As long as he kept within the law, he had key qualities for being an excellent business-person.

At times there will be things you need to do to ensure your weaknesses don't get in the way, but without contorting yourself to try and achieve those things. Awareness without judgement means you are in a position to solve your challenges, and make the most of them.

If you are an ideas person, but don't enjoy implementing those ideas, partner with someone who loves implementing and would benefit from an ideas person. If you want a job where you can organise events, find an organisation where other people are working on subjects that would make truly interesting events.

Find a gap where you fit, with others having the jigsaw pieces that complement your skills, pay someone to do the things you hate, or swap with others who have talents that you need and want the help you can offer.

After all, you don't have to be great at everything. We live in a society where individuality is highly valued. We expect ourselves to be extraordinary. Social expectations push us to equate being extraordinary with fame, financial fortune or being at the top of our profession.

The truth is, the people who hit success always have others helping them. Steve Jobs never invented Apple's technology. That was Steve Wozniak. But Steve Wozniak didn't have the business instinct, that was Steve Jobs. When they worked together, Apple Computers was created.

Brene Brown, a leading researcher on connection, shame and vulnerability, says that in the modern world one of the things we have learned to feel ashamed of is feeling we are not 'extraordinary'. By doing this, we devalue our everyday achievements, however hard won they are.

However hard we work at our job, we are not good enough because we are not at the top of the ladder. However wonderful our children are, we are never able to juggle all the expectations around parenting, careers (whether or not we have a job or parent full-time) and having a beautiful home.

There is real value in being who you already are, *whatever* that is.

If trying to be extraordinary brings us shame, a sense of inadequacy and failure, if trying to be extraordinary cuts us off from the people we love, if trying to be extraordinary stops us seeing the riches that we already have, then what value does it really have?

It takes courage to see ourselves as worthy, just as we already are. If we trust that what we offer is enough, that what we are is enough, we can provide the world with the best role model in existence.

Career Change Exercise 18: If You Felt Worthy...

Ask yourself this one question: if you felt worthy, what would you be capable of?

# Chapter 14: Time to discover who you are

*Do I know how yet? No. But I will*

**Bill Baren**

We all need downtime, sometimes, especially as we go through a big life change.

If you don't yet feel clarity about your direction, perhaps you are not yet ready to have that clarity. Sometimes there is more emotional or practical learning to be done first.

Think back to the time you were a teenager. This great big life transition, from childhood to adulthood, probably left you disoriented. You swung between certainty and feeling totally lost. You were influenced by others, because you were not yet certain who you were. You slept a lot because change is exhausting and traumatic.

It is ironic that it is in the midst of this transition that society asks young people to make some of their big life and career decisions, decisions that can affect the rest of their lives. Ironic because in this state of change, you are badly prepared to make this kind of decision.

A similar transition can occur later in life. Some of the common reasons include being made redundant, getting married, becoming a parent, going through a bereavement, getting divorced, moving country... anything that changes your life in such a way that affects your daily routine and an aspect of your identity.

One or more of these events can catalyse a career change. Or they can stop you in your tracks, rendering you incapable of engaging fully in yet another traumatic change. Even if this is so, there are still things you can do to be ready.

Seek out interesting and stimulating experiences to help you learn more about what you love and how to make it happen.

Unhook from the assumption that once you have made a career choice it is set in stone. You can always change direction later (even if you are already 70). Speaking as one who has changed direction many times, each change develops the skills and resourcefulness to get through a change again.

Be kind to yourself and give yourself the space to breathe, the time to recover from shock of whatever else is happening in your life.

Social entrepreneur and founder of *Who Made Your Pants?*, Becky John, described how she gave herself permission one Christmas to take a break and let the answer come to her about what she wanted to do. By the end of that time she had made the decision. She had committed herself to starting her social enterprise and it started to take on its own momentum - its own life.

But even before she made the commitment to the social enterprise, she had made a commitment to herself. A commitment to take the space to make the decision.

Contemplation time is not the same as feeling stuck. When we are stuck we avoid looking at ourselves, what we want and what we might change.

When we contemplate, we make a commitment to ourselves. We commit to giving ourselves space. We commit to taking the emotional risk of really looking. While we may not be ready to decide on a particular course of action, but we commit to respecting ourselves and the decision enough to give it our attention.

Career Change Exercise 19: Making Space to Look

Sit with your Love It List and your list of skills, and enjoy them, without feeling the pressure to decide, yet, what they might lead to. Notice how you feel about making the commitment to yourself, trusting that the answer will come.

Notice what seems really important to you right now. Notice what is possible for you if you have the space to contemplate it.

If you are indecisive by nature, you might want to put a limit on your contemplation time. The limit might also help you to really honour the time you need, to really stop and not fill it with activity.

You might also want to clarify for yourself what you need before you can make a decision. Do you need to speak to your partner, write a plan or do some research? If so, do it as part of your contemplation.

Letting yourself off the hook to make the change right now is not the same as giving up on your dream. The opposite is true. It gives you the space for the dream to develop while you also develop your ability to make it the dream happen. Stay faithful to the dream and allow the answers to come to you when you are ready.

Bill Baren, who I quoted at the beginning of this chapter, once spoke of his own vision on a webinar I listened to.

I loved Bill's faith, his peace with the idea that he would get there. It spoke to me of a confidence that if he continued on his life's path - seeking out what had most meaning for him, serving the people he felt he was there to serve and seizing opportunities to learn and grow wherever he finds them – if he does those things, it would, inevitably, lead him to achieve what he truly desired.

So, don't worry about doing everything right now. Slow down and taste the riches of the place you already are. Connect with people (including yourself) and see where it takes you. Allow yourself to be a *witness* to who you really are.

If you don't know the answers, start by trusting that you will, when the time is ripe. Move and learn in tune with your values, but don't wait for the perfect answer to fall into your lap.

Building in space and opportunities to notice what really matters, who you are and what you want. These are ingredients for a fulfilling life.

# Chapter 15: Bringing it all together

*You know you're in love when you can't fall asleep*
*because reality is finally better than your dreams*

**Dr. Seuss**

In this book we have been working on giving you clarity about what motivates you to work in a third sector organisation, what abilities you have to offer that you really enjoy and what environment brings our your best.

Write on your chart your top three skills. Use your most resonant passions from your Love It List to come up with up to three possible career ideas (even if you are not sure if they exist) and put them in your ideas list on the chart.

Be creative. Put your skills and motivations to come up with new ideas.

For example, if you like mentoring and graphic design, and want to help elderly people feel less lonely, then how about teaching web design to retired people so they can volunteer and offer their design skills to local charities.

Or if you love Liverpool, cats and investment, perhaps you are ideally suited to finding social investment opportunities for cat charities in that city.

It is possible that these ideas won't pan out. But combining your skills and motivations in these ways can open your mind to ideas that do work, and for which you are uniquely suited. And if you don't find they already exist, you may discover an idea for a social enterprise that really works.

Remember Becky John, founder of *Who Made Your Pants?*

She combined her love of nice lingerie, her hate of waste and her desire to employ disadvantaged women into a social enterprise and won the Lloyds Bank and Bank of Scotland Social Entrepreneur of the Year Award in 2014. The business is run as a co-operative, employing refugee women who create beautiful lingerie made from the waste offcut material from the fashion industry. Their pants are beautiful. I wear them myself.

Even if you identify as a renaissance person, pick no more than three job ideas for now to work on and explore. This is more effective than trying to develop ten new careers at once. Remember, you can always print off more copies of the chart and develop your other ideas later. This is not about limiting your future.

You may be feeling butterflies in your tummy as you tune into your real motivations and values.

You will want to stay in touch with that resonance as you communicate with potential employers. Because being in love, even if it is in love with your own career ideas, is magnetic.

Think about a time when you have spoken to a person who loves what they do and knows why it matters. Moving, isn't it?

It is moving for a potential employer too. Remember that as you start to research and apply for the jobs that truly suit you.

# Chapter 16: Next steps

*Take your life in your own hands and what happens? A terrible thing: no one to blame.*

**Erica Jong**

This book is all about discovering who you are and what kind of work you feel motivated by. Now you need to find and get that job.

Now that you know what you want to pursue, that may be easy. For many people, gaining the clarity and determination is the toughest bit.

But if you are someone who knows what they want, but not how to go about finding it, my upcoming books many help

In March 2015 I will be publishing *The Ethical Career Guide* on Kindle.

*The Guide* starts where this book finishes. It takes what you know about yourself and teaches you how to find the kind of employers you'd really like to work for, get to know the sector better and understand its challenges, rewards and jargon well enough to speak like an insider.

In April 2015, the third book in the series, *Good Job Hunting* is launched. This book is about the nitty gritty of actually getting the job you want. It covers applications, interviews and how to get access to the hidden jobs market: the vast number of jobs that are never advertised at all.

Finally, in June 2015, keep your career change moving with the *Career Motivation Toolkit*. Feel yourself flagging, procrastinating or avoiding the pain of change? This book is full of tools and tips to keep you on track, while staying sane.

You will also find a wealth of free resources: articles, podcasts and videos, to help you find a fulfilling ethical career at www.mynewleaf.co.uk.

If you want someone who walk beside you, guiding and cheering you on your way as you make your own career change, you can find out more about individual non-profit career coaching there too.

I offer a free initial consultation to people who are serious about their career change. You can apply by emailing devi@mynewleaf.co.uk

Worried about whether I am going to be the right coach for you? The consultation gives you a taster to help you decide. I choose a coach if I spot three things about them:

Firstly, the things they say inspire me, or remind me of what I know to be important. In other words, they feel resonant.

Secondly, the idea of working with them excites me and slightly scares me. I know they are going to push me out of my comfort zone, but only as far as I can manage.

Finally, they have experience of helping others get results and can talk about that confidently. If you ask, they should also be able to give you the contact details of past clients who can testify to that.

Remember, making a change takes time, so work with people who are going to commit to working with you over a period of months and in the way that works for you.

## About the Author

Devi Clark has a postgraduate Diploma in Careers Guidance from the University of East London (QCG), is a Certified Professional Co-active Coach (CPCC) with the Coaches Training Institute and has an MA in English Literature and History from the University of Edinburgh.

Devi moved from a management career in a FTSE 100 company when she realised that she wanted to help people do what really matters to them, rather than following a conventional path. For ten years she has provided careers guidance and social enterprise start up advice to people who want to find a career that makes a difference while earning them a living.

She has worked with refugees and asylum seekers, residents of Tower Hamlets and more recently with any individual who want to find a meaningful ethical career.

Devi also works as a third sector management consultant, including strategy, business and project development, grant fundraising and project evaluation. She enjoys coaching leaders in small & medium sized charities & social enterprises; people who, like her, combine management excellence with a social vocation.

Find out more about Devi and her work at www.mynewleaf.co.uk

Printed in Great Britain
by Amazon